IN THE FUTURITY LOUNGE

IN THE FUTURITY LOUNGE

ASYLUM FOR INDETERMINACY

POEMS

Marjorie Welish

COFFEE HOUSE PRESS

MINNEAPOLIS

2012

COPYRIGHT © 2012 by Marjorie Welish
COVER DESIGN by Linda Koutsky
AUTHOR PHOTOGRAPH © Star Black

Coffee House Press books are available to the trade through our primary distributor, Consortium Book Sales & Distribution, cbsd.com. For personal orders, catalogs, or other information, write to: Coffee House Press, 79 Thirteenth Avenue NE, Suite 110, Minneapolis, MN 55413.

Coffee House Press is a nonprofit literary publishing house. Support from private foundations, corporate giving programs, government programs, and generous individuals helps make the publication of our books possible. We gratefully acknowledge their support in detail in the back of this book.

Good books are brewing at coffeehousepress.org

LIBRARY OF CONGRESS CIP INFORMATION
Welish, Marjorie, 1944–
In the futurity lounge : asylum for indeterminacy /
by Marjorie Welish.
p. cm.
ISBN 978-1-56689-302-2 (alk. paper)
I. Title.
PS3573.E4565 I47
811'.54—dc22
2011029280

FIRST EDITION | FIRST PRINTING
1 3 5 7 9 8 6 4 2
PRINTED IN THE USA

ACKNOWLEDGMENTS

Some of these poems appeared originally in the following publications: *Bomb, Boston Review, Chicago Review, Conjunctions, Critical Quarterly* [U.K.], *Fence, Jacket, Notre Dame Review, Parataxis, This Corner* [U.K.], *VLAK* [Prague], and *War and Peace*. A special thanks goes to Jean-Jacques Poucel and to *Double Change*.

The author is grateful for the support of the New York Foundation for the Arts in the writing of this book.

IN THE FUTURITY LOUNGE

IN THE FUTURITY LOUNGE

IN THE FUTURITY LOUNGE

SPACING

AND IT CAME TO PASS

that the King died; then the Queen died of grief.

CONSEQUENTS UNITE!

And the Queen died of grief, chafing against the antecedent

event, action, scene. And again the Queen died

in line, and so consecutive with respect to others who had died

prior to her.

IT GOES WITHOUT SAYING

that the Queen died.

ONCE UPON A TIME

is of a different order of magnitude, the Donor said.

CONSECUTIVE STUDIOS

Valiant folding screens doubling back to distinguish COMPLETE from COMPLETED

strike at anthology's information and friends, countless EXHAUST in debt to EXHAUSTIVENESS

EXHAUSTIVENESS INCONCLUSIVE. It is midnight. Modern signage and settings

in legendarily discrepant turf. "We walk past a storefront." What is knowledge

to them who have it? The lower portion falling back selectively, and/or idiomatically

omnivorous: the wall.

EXTREME PUBLIC SPACE

SUNDAY the supplement has now molted *SUNDAY*: A huge sheet within which unfolded

his retrospective dissimilar and unequal and nonpareil.

Proceeding to the next

anthology's EXHAUSTIVENESS for an INCONCLUSIVE public, we are made late. Doubling back

across validity is this self. The TABLE OF CONTENTS "from top to bottom or from bottom to top"

indicates a prospectus of stoppages, a sketch that takes time distributes a serious attempt we read as

a built statement. In its wake, the sentence . . .

An anthology's EXHAUSTIVENESS, INCONCLUSIVE

entablature: completed not complete, not completed complete, not completed not complete,

completed complete.

Exhaustively happy, we open out the graphic

sonogram of the event that is the storefront, red and black.

IN SITU

HERE LIE

THE FALLEN

Here lie the fallen phrasings of

exemption and non-exemption

Here lies the fallen phrasing of

commemorative writing on behalf of

exemption and non-exemption

without which and without whom

THIS CERTIFIES THAT

This certifies that writing so named

was completed in accordance with

programmed guy wires with/without

naming undertaken in fact yet

as agreed as described

FOUND

Road under purse allowing the debut of coins

the debit of its mouth

ROAD OPEN

to mouth at or on coins, road rolling under

A lay purse, mouth open, let out a coin

LOST? PLACED?

A coin toss

well-informed as to time, sequence, and location

DATED MATERIAL

If you are currently receiving

if you do not receive

valid through

validate by

a lingering taste

Of discursive space the color of substrate: Start

from rent: THIS IS A NON-EVICTION PLAN

NO NON-RESIDENTIAL PURCHASING TENANT

WILL BE EVICTED—and continue as you were

brushing off the sand, blowing off

the circumstantial him- or her- self

drawn up the ramp of

4

ASSEMBLY

How could you put forth a plan for
Even as he was uncertain
As pressure mounts on
To give better cause

How could you put forth half
In announcing the spread of
Sound, they from other sources?

EXIT

He fell perfectly. Without property.
He fell immanently. He did not fall. He felt
that: to what does this refer? Please get up

in thresholds to speak with eras—
and haltingly in the units of periphery
pursuant to multiplicities.

VACATE

On one hand
on the other

NOTICE

A small aperture encounters intensities

seizing words and bed

UNDER NEW OWNERSHIP

and bed mussed then unmade

then composed then fabricated then

improved then abducted then

remembered then performed then

FIGURE

The poet redirected my likeness.

She said, "Not his decadence, which is a question."
"Time," she said, declining his epidemic.

                                   As if serrated,

initiatives lost modernity: aura reared up
although bracketing pages in comparative matters.

                                              "What time is it?"

                                                      "Perspectivism."

Which is a question.

                    As if serrated,

"as if" bracketing pages.

And time again, the timing of a wrecking ball—

                                        Which is an overture.

STATEMENT
(SOME ASSEMBLY REQUIRED)

The real

       kept public has caught a sliver of interim, alarms coincident

with honking: the ambulance cut short in its path, stranded in logic spaced thus—includes a sample

of Sufi calligraphy from the XVI century affixed to Mughal court paper in the XVII century—the seam

between stares.

       PLEASE TEAR ALONG PERFORATION between this wet refreshed axis

and adjusted reading.

       Honking worth discussing.

The real

       kept pace with the axis for realpolitik, not the least site of which is the metropolis

virtual through and through: instanced are the atria disproportionate to scuffs eastbound. The

wayfaring stranger is obsolete, try diaspora upon diaspora through the drive-through ventilator

and the logic spaced thus.

       A quantity of it, drive by/drive-in INTERMISSION of the built, and

at the bar, I called for the realpolitik of utopia.

The real

       kept beeping calligraphy to cut an infill between stares and the asterisk—for the Indian

collector of Iranian descent to PRESS FIRMLY where etiquette goes. Or can we speak to early

ambulances compatible with patronage,

       the tile behind

you and the car brakes?

The real

        kept pace with the splay of wall, walk-in and walk-through and walk-by—a
perfect if small inscription.

                A sliver of invented speech. To disrupt speaking, you're interrupting
architecture with foreground again.

The real

        cut a surfeit of area such that paradise attributed to, in the circle of, school of, is flood we
read now.

        Calligraphy cut itself. The storefront on the left or the right.

TO BE CONT.

A turnstile for . . .

an incision

a LION

a folie (mindful of that elevated Parc de la Villette), derives its altitude from
the tracks: interleaved with overgrowth, a concrete walk that ramifies now
and then in spots and at edges to allow for plants to remain interleaved with
pedestrian path even as transplanted locales and some trees create flanking
borders the length of the line; some narrow slatted benches rising from
cantilevered concrete also express the line, split and ramified, to install all
social and natural structural function.

A LION

. . . insofar as they solved the problem of retaining the sense of
wildness while accommodating the pedestrian traffic, traffic that
would obviously have ruined the growth if . . .

Laying bare the rail

laying bare the rain

Pointing to the traffic, the frame; meanwhile the LION rescues the pedestrian
(the LION rescues the liar) and dead end where a spur now allows idling

10

above traffic. Please be Seated. PLEASE BE SEATED. Extrude bench from
floor, render verisimilitude of platform for Standing Walking Sitting and of
Lying laid bare in said versatility of bench to raise flooring to beach language
now locked into position. Versatility of referring . . .

WILDERNESS. He wrote LOOK but DO NOT TOUCH concerning this.
Since pedestrians would kill . . .

the grassy WATERFRONT

already deviating from space as it accommodates the preexisting non-identity of . . .

. . . avenue through the constructed fraying of walk, and transition is constant
is a constant path is not as straight as the rail line itself but "weaves"
interweaves its functions WALK DON'T WALK

immobilizing incision?

The gift of no destination is. Strolling is as was an urban substitute for walking to and from.

And yet he was sent to the gulag for looking up from under . . .

Scripted space did/did not affront you, Beauty locked/unlocked Truth
locked/unlocked and intimated floor, which is the spur for seating the SUN meanwhile unlocks.

Walk but not seamlessly. You are not pretending to be nature the garden pretends
but this garden professes textual strategy of a post-structural
repetition following the . . . the railroad itself transposed the avenue.
Constructed fraying of walk and WALK AND DON'T WALK, BUILT as a constant.

11

Lying on the bare flooring locked/unlocked sun; intimated from floor was
Beauty unlocked and extruded. Beauty extruded a spur for seating; the SUN
meanwhile goes languorous now that it is disused—no, it goes as it went
aggregating patches of grid . . . ng the preexisting non-identity of . . .

Occluded folie. Occluded folie temporarily.

A turnstile

was railroad then undergrowth, then overgrowth revealed a prospect. TO BE
CONTINUED. Plot from dereliction: a garden. Create scenic spot from
derelict zone. Create beauty free/not free of modest/immodest free/determinate but
modest when compared with . . .

not poor in referring.

SPASM FOR WALL

Supported by a stolid scythe-bearer, a gamin dressed in seismic shocks and tics conveys the relevance of modern dance as sign.

As against experience.

Leaning against experience appearing to leaning against the sign of wall.

The scythe-bearing sign unperturbed by tics and shocks breathing the air.

Ionization by Edgard Varèse shall have been traffic by now.

Apron or no apron, apron (black) shifted to the hip of the skirt (red) of the scythe-bearer's counterpart.

The pair paced itself to synchronized counters such as arms admitting left and right to go abroad

Out into the traffic paces the scythe-bearer.

Annul wall with prompt.

Peering or peeping she fingers the differential of wall-within-wall then explicates this slide as divergent bed for rewarding the body.

In spasm, the full extent of the cross-section.

INTERIOR

ALL INTERIM IS (*Julius Caesar*)—

overcast axe

        or figure

        as the mount without its display

of injury, entirely informed by it.

                How

is knowledge tried through the enthymeme

                    in which he appears?

Hinged walls rot

hinged wls rotate

hinged walls, both axes

experimental jade axis

           is a thing

yet it is a thing of grammar.

MEANWHILE pamphlet

           reads it *to the city outside.*

DEXTROUS

1

The poet has the same name as the conspirator, a scene
from within. LET THEM DIVIDE transparency from translucency and indecency,

Brutus, the making of modernity, some say, whose
after-hours flashbacks prove new civil wars—1848 given
to originate one anthology of primary sources, 1890 given
to invite cities of other, in secondary sources—whose

death? Week 1: Skepticism, or Who Knows What? The object
with standard staples: writing to be looked at, drawing to be read

in opaque questionnaires: WHAT DO I KNOW? obliges our doubling back to fractional
skepticism toward normative universal attempts: FOLD HERE. Deaths
laying flat that era EXEUNT SEVERALLY.

2

Of writing legible but not intelligible: reverse obliges us to
read the seeing. Of turning then this opacity
translucent transparency scored for the distribution of

writing. Insert double fold whose deed it is
TO JOIN THEM and their signature

to a set of written interstices a set of edges . . . deaths
[words blotted out] to be looked at as is

the invoice: Week 1: Skepticism, or Who Knows What? The object

created of illocutionary force obliges the double fold

for interpreting the proposition MODERNITY, in whose name . . .

Note the confrontation with Cinna in what seems to be a trivial scene,

after the [words missing] the debate between

Brutus and Anthony, inheritors of the name WHO GOES THERE?

FOLD HERE. Deaths laying flat the era EXEUNT SEVERALLY.

3

The poet has the same name as the conspirator, a scene

from within. LET THEM DIVIDE transparency from translucency and indecency,

of a fact

without its narrative

the author of *Axel's Castle*

decoding the soon-to-be-normative moderns

through symbolist volition: to-do-or-not taxonomy of 1890.

Your overlay struck territory onto the chart the large glass in manifesto and executive bodies

BACKSLASH, the markings of modernity, some say, UNDERSCORE after-hours flashbacks,

hair-trigger civil wars—should I write that?

DILUTE the anthology of 1848 given

CONDENSE the autobiography of 1890 given

to invite cities or to invite THE CITY

He reversed my question or questionnaire: "So then, the AVANT-GARDE need not be
a collective that puts art in the service of social revolution; it could conceivably be
disengaged socially but engaged aesthetically."

FOLD HERE. Deaths laying flat that era EXEUNT SEVERALLY.

SKEPTICISM VS. INCREDULITY

Q. Marjorie, is this a Rembrandt?

A. Nothing disallows its being a Rembrandt.

UNLIKE HIS FRIEND

RESET "want to prevent"

PAUSE
PAUSE "want to learn"
ENACT "want to bring about"

START "wants to marry"

RESET "want to prevent" convalescence

PAUSE
PAUSE "want to learn" convalescence
ENACT "want to bring about" convalescence

START "wants to marry" convalescence

RESET "want to prevent". . . *more concerned to probe knowledge than is Oppen (who recoils from knowledge as much as Zukofsky is drawn to it); Oppen discards forms of formal education. His was another way, through the songs of first-hand experience, rather.*

PAUSE
PAUSE "want to learn" *formal education. His was another way, to pass through the songs of first-hand experience.*

ENACT "want to bring about" . . . *more concerned to probe knowledge than is Oppen (who recoils from knowledge as much as Zukofsky is drawn to it);*

START "wants to marry" *of formal education. His was another way, through the songs*

19

FOR BEST RESULTS, TRY . . .

. . . sound of street sweeper accompanying sight of school bus traveling down Ninth Avenue.

Woman waiting, man entering right; woman exiting left.

Brecht: men rowing, side-by-side.

Man reading on bench removes himself to next bench, looks back at bench as if to explain
that the sun, not my presence, caused his move.

Side-by-side.

Or that I had wanted to compare Barrett Watten's "Three" with Brecht's "Conversations
Rowing" (trans. Edwin Morgan) but had not the time to do so.

End.

Or that non-identity offers an alternative to the reciprocity with which Brecht's
"Conversations Rowing" endows a type.

What is China?

If (Watten's) "Footnote to Tibet" is structuralist, "China" reserves a sociolect. Perelman's
"China"'s China is orientalist even to itself, in paper stock and typeface that make albums
arcades of self-presentation.

Not, non-, un-being, render states incommensurable.

China stares at a wall.

End.

American ending: Elderly woman wheeling shopping cart sits down.

She wears sunglasses, the frames of which construct 2-0-0-9.

. . . sits down, gets up, walks away.

Perelman stares at a wall. China

wears sunglasses, the frames of which construct 2-0-0-9.

Tibet, reading on bench removes itself to next bench, looks back at bench as if to explain

       that the sun, not my presence, caused its move.

Watten sits down, gets up, walks away.

Perelman is orientalist even to himself.

In paper stock and typeface, Watten.

China makes arcades of self-representation.

Tibet is album entitled "Footnote to Tibet."

What is China?

Perelman reading on bench removes himself to the next bench.

Watten looks back at bench as if to explain.

Tibet caused his move.

Tibet, non-, un-being.

Perelman's "China" renders states incommensurable.

Watten's Tibet endows a type with non-identity

       alternative to non-being—a kind of reciprocity.

China sits down, gets up, walks away.

Or that I had wanted to compare

a man with man, rendering states incommensurable.

Shall I compare thee, sound of street sweeper, to an accompanying sight of school bus?
China, and China in diaspora even to itself.

Or that you had wanted to mention
                the drama of repairing a small tool—*Don't explain*
self to self, rather start a kind of reciprocity:
the drama of a small tool repairing large machinery.
Man on bench removes himself to the next bench and she removing unmentionables:
                leaf blowers.

Or that you were repairing yourself with a small tool
                even as she applied scolding
to the poetics of auto parts in the company of flashing school buses.
All this time women have been reading "China" through the surplus,
a surfeit of horizons, differing with respect to the sun.

Materials mention genuine supplies.
Uncollected sound, sounds sounding out terrain
in paper stock and typeface that make albums arcades of self-presentation.
Don't mention it! Yellow school buses

accompanied by the street sweeper are becoming amplified through her lenses
even as she scolds us in paper stock and typeface.
    . . . *rue with a difference* and being render states incommensurable.
The sun removes itself to the next bench as she removes unmentionables: aerosol.

Plain as that we had wanted comparative literature for the million,
photo albums have been reading "China" as surplus.
She wears a small tool with a difference discord departure divergence,
                the frames of which construct 2-0-0-9.
    . . . sits down, gets up, walks away.

22

ADVERT

1

        That year dress supposed open-source

stenciling onto fabric as in the manner of
                EXHAUST.

At ALL: The will to acquire
           INTEREST
                on Earth

and inhabit
       a following
           for the left hand.
                A disciple

removed THIRSTY? from the PROTEST!
                Preface

OBJECT
       operating the book
           on Earth—

and LIPS
      TO INTENSIFY THE INCENTIVE

on the theory that it was a directive not a question.
                THIRSTY?

Devoted to YOUR THIRST

                  obedient

OBEY YOUR THIRST for FOLLOW YOUR THIRST

cursively across the body

                up to and including SUBMIT TO OUR THIRST,

devours saying translated from the American brand.

                        Another diagnostic:

ATTAIN TO CLOSING THAT BOOK

                    involving acts of open-source

fabric as in the manner of

doubt

        TRANSLATED FROM the American dawn.

                  A disciple

removed THIRSTY? from the signage

on the theory that it was a directive not a question.

Assuming both a directive and a question

                  he followed daylight

through the labyrinth.

Unlocated and redubbed, the labyrinth's

yawn.

     An accomplice removed THIRSTY? from

                  the novella, the novella's warm nights.

An intern staved off small change.
The helper tattooed small change on the theory that THAT'S THAT.

STALK YOUR MOTH

2

     That year dress involved acts of EXHAUST
open-source and/or public onto fabric in the manner of goth

At ALL: The will to acquire

          INTERDICTION

              on Earth

and inhabit it

     gaudily if not presumptively.

          FOR THE LEFT HAND.

Flirtations removed THIRSTY? from PROTEST

          —a diversionary tactic preface

to holiday,

      operating the book

            on Earth—

and LIPS

      WEDDED TO A SMILE.

Devoted to YOUR THIRST

          obedient

OBEY YOUR THIRST in testaments

cursively across the body

          up to and including LEASE OUR THIRST,

devour sayings intercepted on the terrace.

            Another diagnostic:

ATTAIN TO CLOSING THAT BOOK

          involving acts of fabric

against nature in the manner of

doubt

      OUTSOURCED from the American dawn.

A devotee

of sea breezes removed virtuosity from the signage

on the theory that it was a directive not a question.

IN DEBT?

The will to acquire but not to do.

The will not to acquire and

THAT'S THAT.

3

That year dress involved acts of fatigue EXHAUST

open-source surplus and/or emitting vapors infinitely theatrical just this side of disgusting

At ALL: The will to exile be outcast yet exclusively

EX OFFICIO

on earth

INHALE BEQUEST

FOR THE LEFT HAND.

APPLESAUCE!

6. *v. assume, usurp, arrogate; get, under false pretenses, said under false colors; encroach infringe, trench on; violate, do violence to; stretch or strain a point, give an inch and take an ell; exact, impose; claim, etc.* (demand) 924.7; *appropriate, seize, etc.* (take) 789.7-9.

THIS AGAINST WHICH

PURSUANT TO

"He means well" is useless unless he does well. —PLAUTUS

You must take the will for the deed. —SWIFT

STRUT YOUR NARCOTIC

PURSUANT TO

moth and rust

moth and rashness

Yes. Such is the toxicological bold stroke

A litigant removed rashness from the blond's fist

PURSUANT TO

a revolving door's conquering where and to whom

                                              occupants build sentences and

episodes

a bypass populated of conquest, and permitting

                                      second thoughts

sieve at nothing.

                    As the half-meant stranger

you became our way out yet data to further

                                penumbra of the unsolid

cabinet

        after the war.

Stick and nothing, wrote someone, probably an understudy

for a Situationist, a Situationist's extra.

                              The entire sample

says CHOOSE YOUR POISON: work for yourself or work for others.

                                            The way

lesser song outmaneuvered the ground,

                        the prosepoem flashed

                                        a stench

the subject expected the object

the object was himself although he did not know it.

HUNT TOO MUCH

IN THE FUTURITY LOUNGE
IN THE FUTURITY LOUNGE

1

No depth meant. Stealth attributed

as silhouetted against orange shadows: orange shadows officiated

incline, slope, ramp, and crevice into which habitués

sat or sit, might have

styled themselves, typing in the vicinity of an idea whose technologies have
        extruded a pause.

The zone voted. An object works. Walk-in signage is suffused with

the floor plan planted in the floor-through floor not unlike

paper. YOU ARE HERE, with the plan, the plan's countryside

co-existing with the plan's latitudes. DESCRIBE TWO MOMENTS.

And having departed from the typewriter,

no chair

is to be found.

2

And having departed from the typewriter

the song stylist has timed out.

But here's the

walk-in signage, where architecture had been;

orange code for each function: entrance/exit, computer station, lavatory, hearth, other?[1]

floor plan, a diagram, embedded in floor at entrance, giving symbolic orientation to . . .

postmodernism for which the visitor is keyed to meaning as the guide was not. Meaning, or
       metalanguage?

differential in floor plane: slope, incline, ramp, terrace, crevice, niche; fluidity of functional
       structure;

noise: human clutter underestimated, semiotic rheostat dimming;[2]

alterations: made to improve convenience and safety but expressed as interference;[3]

writing: verbal model presupposed in conceptual art.[4]

---

[1] color is intelligible here as signage only insofar as one realizes that color is information.

[2] people and their stuff not entirely factored in; and was the gift shop anticipated?

[3] barrier set "temporarily" on rim of slightly terraced ramp, for instance.

[4] key terms for functional aids meant to substitute for structural self-evidence in a post-analytic
   theory of architecture.

3

X *cannot come today but will come tomorrow*

always

keeping the promise

on ramp or ramparts.

Grave inscription: ENTER

SAME grave

inscription

on ramp or ramparts—no, I take it back–size and shape are to be found only there
where all proclamations descry screens

below grade

step on stepping stones, winding stairs together with at least two exits, and ramp conforming

to the building code, send subject on a quest for

orange wariness, hunted bird

with wire

boar with covered pit

rabbit with children's book

SAME contract

on ramp or ramparts—no, I take it back–size and shape are to be found only there
where all proclamations descry screens

on which to type themselves—

the forces of

orange are at work! Hearth and lavatory glow as they rotate

at a speed of one revolution per day

in velocities velo cities, as Velamir is a fast-moving person
so futurity tailgates the past, peels rubber. V. disbelieved acceleration

> as relative

> and so

was pulled down by it

> rose-tinted.

4

Nocturnal typewriter extruded. With chair throughout, air underneath—creating a dispute,
in shadow, encountering

> you intercepted, a chair typed

and paper swollen with amphitheater's engorged shadow
in the vicinity of an idea.

> Steal away.

The zone voted. An object works. Walk-in signage aflame with proclivities
not unlike an incline deferred

> or a pause that inherits a stop.

View radiator. YOU ARE HERE, with the heat, the heart's launch
coexisting with health's per diem. DESCRIBE TWO MOMENTS.

> And having departed from

the typewriter (Smith-Corona declares bankruptcy in 1995) the documentary meant other
> future perfect

maths (28,000 B.C.E., Europeans notch and tally)

Early (in 1938 the Biro brothers put out the first ballpoint) remainder

Earlier firm evidence that

Earliest the first the first-known knowable fire

View radiator: YOU, a milieu for which HERE is a launch, poster, placard

                                                  my standard

territory *even when they tear up their own posters.* Tear up their future perfect

                                                           fire. PLEASE POST

Earliest known future perfect

IN THE FUTURITY LOUNGE (DETAIL)

Earlier firm evidence that

In the event that

A fact ignited our perfected enthusiasm, roseate guesses and

      graphics through which we exited

First fact

Advent of fact

meets problematic, foliage for an underground set beneath a provident

      blaze of corrugated

space-time HERE premature,

                                  preliminary to a nice onset of popularity

and neo-vague agog.

Prior to eclipse:

                 advent of the new vague (human) agog and (avian) silence

YOU

    facial

        fall salient

Earliest the first the first-known knowable fire

Earlier than today

Early green

SUBJECT MATTER

He walks does not walk to the stump. He sets does not set a microphone on the stump—interesting here is some bread we are out of bread and while you're at it would you prefer controversy can you spare stationary nature he said placing a rotary fan where the microphone had been a lure. A carpenter's level on a huge screen fluorescent sounds finish the aural amphitheater. Car alarm. And steering wheel for the tree and tree canopy a kind of wrapping paper or coat hanger. He will teach architects about sentences: Stein and her car alarm. He will or will not. He would unfold the sound system unfold the monochrome microphone tapping graph paper he would lay a sentence speaking across the microphone not into it about the lay of the land then he would lay the land on the scape slipped under the campus as it is to be. Coat hangers and vocations. He points to the factor then the entity then the item. If it were the 1970s he would have hung the microphone from a tree limb letting it swing, but it is the Sixties. The microphone tips over crushes the graph paper with a loud roar the sea uncrushes it sand lays upon a fresh sheet of graph paper. It must be the Sixties he says to himself I should have foreseen that rolling his sleeves raveling the extension cord.

To see change it from active to constative he writes on page 25 the leaves drying the leaves drying fall out as we walk under or among (amongst) or past for past language (before XII c.) or amongst languages See FOLIAGE then See LAMINA not the same "see" in the sense of "refer to" the foliage consult the "representation of leafage (as in architecture)" fell to a fault as Beckett does and does not. Leafage leapt from the wall sprung from her thigh not the same manufacture had a propensity to dry wet each at differing rates of leakage occurring within a spectrum or scale scar scarred limits apparent why not fall Beckett asks sand from rock to gravel to sand strongly marked and or play again The sea uncrushes the sheet See LAMINA pulverizes it "thinner than foil" Electroplate the reader with sights and sounds.

MATTER IN HAND

More specifics

legible, capable of being read charismatically, if unintelligibly writ
or written intelligibly lenient *despite indistinctness or obscurity*
since reversed: inverted involved upside down scrambled sampled and
      put through a sieve crushed with the blade of a knife cubed
      and quartered split off from plaintext
yet easy enough to identify as language.
As "involute" is *shrinking or returning to its former size*
      or as regressive as part of the aging process
and as "involve" is a warrant to roll up or wrap *to engage as a participant*
      to oblige to take part, envelop entail and to cling in principle
      that grammar *the insertion of clauses between subject and predicate*
so, lag delay and slow as shine accrues to leather paths through undisclosed leaf and ditch
      some backwardness

that started us breathing graphics
and noise as the translucent scroll decelerated
to inscriptions to be looked at
diagrams to be read, throughout a studio
of interpolated chaos. *Even more fascinating*
is fig. 59.
      Untranslatable but not at all points
is the posthumous overlay.

ROEBLING ROPE

1

Wiring river—river wired above murderous logs—

in a concomitant remedy, we are traversing a purpose

                                           with another purpose

reinventing the river below.

                            WIRE: SUSPEND AQUEDUCT

as xylem to a system. THIS WAY *to move stacks* toward a reality towed uphill a patent

for an abridged syllogism *and being displaceable in opposite directions in a timed*

             reciprocating manner to move stacks toward each other's concept.

                                          Hemp

hauling water against gravity

                        frays, breaks help.

                                ENTER wire rope whose cross-section is

THIS WAY

POSTED water

                 above the exposed river traffic floundering once beside a landscape pulled

                        through

an anthem that built the channel above the cause, he said, in possession of an exit.

                          A RAFT OF SOCIAL HISTORY

                          REPOSES HERE

2

We are traversing frayed help

                  with another fraught help, commemorative

we are traversing a wire with know-how we fortify a wire with the advent of scale

how we fortify wire with the twill principle, reaping ardor

                              with another

freaked river decanted to a point in cross section a cantilever first suspension

river becomes an event then and in retrospect as a past enlarged in wetness

for a past and signage now wet and as a panorama diminishing

to a crunch viewed by wet pedestrians who will have been elements.

Decanted to a pointing cross-section above the fray

                              is the cause cut at right angle to axis to vent

frameworks for wire rope. A cross-section of the fray is the cause charged then and in

retrospect enlarged strand skein cable hauling gravity cogently and patented

                                  safe conduct as

the knowledge we are traversing. Panoramic diminishing to a commemorative effect

split between forethought and moisture 2,000 tons of it. Remarks further the memorandum.

Sort out the cross purposes in a landmark. Confer knowledge authorize warrant entitle

legitimate rope without stinting cause and effect as charged.

From Scots 13c: LOAD, CARGO.

3

Organizing social forceps the commemorative impulse
circa 1980 does the knowledge, thus specifying 1848
in signage that disinters cultural strata,

                        the freight of the song

Organizing social forceps in signage that disinters
                        the freight of the song

transportation
material science
civil engineering
pragmatic philosophy
patent law

4

Sheer perhaps.

And/or limit conditions of arriving wind . . .

Bundled into strands compacted into cable steadied within helix was remedy.

. . . if aerodynamics for suspension then unknown. Aeolian.

Bundled into strands compacted into cable steadied within helix were wire.

Gravity whose cross-purpose . . .

not want of strength but want of stability aerodynamically.

Past: frayed lopped off sold for firewood.
Wind it through present postlude.

PASTORAL TRANSFUSION

Fallingwater does not seek
protection of a few forsythia.

Torrential utopias on/off
torrential utopias in the eye of the beholder who goes there.
Of audibility's deflected speech
Strindbergian one moment, Brechtian the next.
We look up at the barge
ATLANTIC CEMENT
sayeth the river.
Look at the sign riding low and engendering stain
          whirling zeal whirling ledges
the likes of which part, the likes of which
part unquenched, unquestioned—or nearly lovely
ledges do stunts, springing water tables and architecture.
Water authenticates the staging area
for an entire environment
of unannihilated possibility up to and including print
          and reading itself.
Canal adumbrates sump, culvert, intertext.
Electrifying earthwork!
Backlog of forgotten songs.
We, the entablature
Shakespearean one moment, Schwittersesque the next.
And so the conservancy seeks a watershed narrative
          to caution against the eye merely.

Scenic commotion meets cantilevering and or not

now issuing from a ledge or ledger and his finger irrigating "R."

Let's go. (They do not move.)

A slap's circumstantial flesh tones

are lost, dissipated into breezes, forgotten songs.

Sounds that heapeth into breezes or recoil from a hard slab

in the eye of the beheld, are the way things are, Cosmos.

As LION is.

Slab!

ONLY ONCE MORE THAT SOAP

LATER THAT DAY

House leaves home. House as proverb
alleges Portikus is folkloric
commentary. *The second bird*
all day long. I used to go
but now, endeavoring
about this, about this thing,
think the woodcut it becomes.
Scenographic booking,
we are here folding sun
into project space, space
where Frankfurt-am-Main had
suspension of saying.

ALBUM, C. 1930

Set to noon. Exile work station, shadow cafeteria, sever lavatory.

Rend cafeteria, dismantle lavatory, wedge work station into wall,

slide cafeteria below grade, raise up garden—the basics

did write it, did stretch, did redact

stuttering in some small way

as of the future. He said that K was not yet, was both

himself and catastrophe, weightless

sentencing and "'wrong' words"

where poems once were.

     All K and leaning on dizziness.

IN AND OUT: the guts. A reduction stuck

stuttering to some small way, unstuck a metropolis

from the wall of sordid expenditure

disguised as stills from old movies in which the quays

stumble but impending night is "funny, sensual, macabre, and illuminating"

OR BY APPOINTMENT. A work-in-progress

is not sullen rust of previously the same

rubble, he articulated.

    The "z" of furious geese.

PAVILION FOR CROSS-TRAFFIC

                                        Cut to
credentials updated hurriedly.
And hurrying to keep up is the retrospective
raggled into coming of age.
                                        Fade to
An indefinite studio, streaming quotes: "had his first (ever?)
exhibition at" cannot be said of bodily processes.
A parenthesis updated:
Do you worry about your archival tapes?
All the time, spake he, from a transverse split gong.

How much? Gusts of
credentials through updated lives.
                                        Cut to
a fade. Memory in her pen inclines
to a retrospective. Arc light! he cried out.

In possession of narrative, gutterals
of a rising curve adjust for surplus space
abundant with sectarian violence;
vilence to parenthesis, our streaming
mistakes should accelerate when run in reverse.
                                        Just think
we shall not have learned anything.
Split between going and coming.

Estimated time: one hour.

LOOSE-FITTING PROOF

In the Age of Steam

... of probability.

Lovely matter.

RE-ENTER

Priority given to enormously long glissandi

the surf shall attempt.

Of blind surfeit baring the device:

seamless extreme

thing punctuated

punched through here and then and

gone and now.

In the Age of Electricity

The great folding doors worked a little more sedately

The great folding ellipse of her face all he could supply

an eclipse to supply brilliant shade.

On the other hand, tea overtakes the cup

Not necessarily, smiles Lewis Carroll
> by way of example.

Off-hand tea overtakes the cup underneath the actuarial table

Railway literature has the tea overtake the actuarial table, dispatching
> Murder and Wedding at once

eclipsing her face.

AN ANTHOLOGY CALLED PEGASUS

Pulse

"... *we were tired of peace.*" And in later cross-traffic
dusty Pleiades hitherto a small modish afterthought.
NOT NOW made of some material.
Matriculated futurity throwing off reflections left and right: Los Angeles.
The hero arrives home unrecognized.

Pulse

That with which a new and selected shelf lets, permits, entreats:
Sand and saw blade—she has bow to blade to breeze and
within a cross-generational miscellany
to alter the perimeters of the object, she, the one and the many.
Recent and raided, opera doing elected battle with itself
while you slow oxen turn the furrowed plain
knowing now, not known then, did know, known and not fallow
known then, but fallow since anomalous.

Pulse

Hawk from a handsaw. TAKE TWO
New and selected melancholia coerced chocolate from delta, keyboard from quay.
The festival opened repeatedly.

New and selective battles cohered to the keep, the keepsake

little performed and so cut from the opera.

The advent of excerpt operated

neon from *ne plus ultra*.

Pulse

This is the anthology for that genealogy. From above and below,

and self-sabotaging disband estates thereof violin's violinist "Problem of the 'Intelligensia'"

(pages 153 ff.) not to recognize self et cetera. But Dada must posit itself

discredited and the city's sentence

"wish-images that take on a revolutionary function are utopia" (page 193)

for which time's punctuality

wanders off the doctrine that is our narrative to ask

nothing, the balconies of.

There is beyond-animal, Pegasus, in a stall of its own.

WANTED:

Zurich at the Cabaret Voltaire on 5 February 1916

vs.

Dada emerged through the antics of multi-lingual bourgeoisie from Eastern Europe who acted on their prerogative as cosmopolites frustrated in their attempt to assimilate into the dominant culture.

Dada began and ended at the Cabaret Voltaire on 5 February 1916. It began and was begun by me at the Cabaret Voltaire on 5 February 1916. Dada began whenever and whether it liked but Dadaism began FOR EXPORT ONLY.

vs.

Dada emerged in fits and starts in dialectical dialect and in trespass of Symbolist property ever more plastic vocables careening from root to ferment in fermented love of ridicule also broke rule to cancel family contract and was exiled exiled himself then to be his own *puer aeternis*. What "not to do next" she conjectured of him befitted transit.

START erupted.

vs.

Break-up of ice then way of life habitually ecstatic. Vehement symposium and/or riot-provoking front-page stress outflanked by the Left.

Wasted in the provinces Dada remained hearsay until witnessed internationally on 5 February 1916 at the Cabaret Voltaire.

vs.

Dada stirred idiosyncratically. Patently never finished emitter of filibuster and backspaces cascading through the loophole provided by the stage grabbed the joke belatedly some say folklore Breton did say translating "to be loved by another."

Dada "was officially christened" on 5 February 1916.

vs.

Yes but.

Everyone knows the line traveling through the lie and this is it: a point the line is alive and this lie is a point—the point. The point of it all is 5 February 1916.

vs.

The six o'clock news is not the point it is a pompom bluff and hedge a pep talk to become knowledge retroactively.

NATURE KNOWS NO FORM AND NO CONCEPTS

vs.

NATURE KNOWS NO FORM AND NO CONCEPTS IS ITSELF A CONCEPT

In the Beginning was Dada!

vs.

Becoming aberrant may have reached a flash point here here and here alternatively might have had here coercively not to mention here and there and May 1915 in diaspora.

You you yo yo you you yo yo—OR ELSE!

vs.

Fright wig yourself!

FLAGS AND THEIR DISCONTENTS

1

Brand name of the ancient city
Your namesake for our ancient city

Ancient unrest and eccentricity
Unrest epitomized by the byte

Even keel immersed in sites
And look: name recognition.

Ancient preferences for ancient
Epiphenomena and nomenclature

Ancient unaccented rubbish
Accented hum of pro and contra

Of dogs' ancient invectives
Of *récits*, abreast of reality.

"Sign no petition."
Underground signs

under the *ancien régime*,
we were initialing entries

lurches and failure: the new state of painting

(read: the new state). Camouflage

to think in asides and aisles, at this stage

employment and deployment ventilated paper

the horizon and the horizon's caricature;

journalists developed a falsetto.

Name it
what's its.

2
Name one
individually named

signboard(s)

named themselves
named by others

unnamed themselves
did not name themselves

historicism

since named

named not yet

does not recognize

the odyssey

charivari   constitutes a kind of primitivism, to which he and they

marginalia   Stephen Rudy's put to chapters

"Dada: A definition," "Dada's Temper" and "Berlin Dada"

index   extracted from the last but for one entry

text   "o. p., 15-, as is," —and I shall speak to this

3

temperature around the edges

temperature at large

temperature by itself

temperature for a variety show

temperature in an unprecedented manner

temperature in his mind

having devalued string

bane disbanded

name Dustbin

"run-on without title breaks, the only indication"

unnamed sources

limped out

R, READING

1

In disorder of appearance:

"151 brutism, simultaneity, spontaneity

154 sound poem

156 Baader

157 Otto Gross"

His sparse occupation of the back cover's everyday

and "technical devices 20" among others taking title

"echoing roots"? Not quite dead yet, garishness

before politics in the realm of a stare—

the logo, the word logo, the word jewel-case

which stuck Dada to its buzz—

providently started negative dialectics penciling

a line drawn, several flagrant diagonals, and a zig-zag laugh.

Meanwhile he added "H" and other found matter.

2

Stephen R R SR udy's marking as heteroglossia to know and to do to not know and to do

etc., (see page 5) avant-garde cut/paste neo-avant-garde's copy/paste dial tone on equivalence

Youth and age aging aged outside, inside a set epithets for the swan also Yeats an apt choice

for studying commutative articles and connectives, for you and she correspond strikingly

A set shirks not
A SET SHIRKS NOT

Optimal conflict for the name at which R—that is to say that R insists that this passage
be what he had not known "Not to have known well enough" snapped to the blank. And so
I left my test bereft.

"Interesting," would be one

A CONCORDANCE OF NEGATION

James's word interesting.

"Not to have known well enough" I thought and believed. Examinations are a test of utmost
possession that admit no guesses, I thought: no fraudulent die the die and its imposter.
I, the rustic.

R read his value drawn in the margin at the words, "learning, a project one endlessly toys
with, and always comes back to"—to know but not to know how to know but not to do as
self-sabotage without knowing it, and other moving edges

MERCE CUNNINGHAM (1919–2009)

SIGNAL TO NOISE

To see, to meet. A formal consultation to obtain information and to evaluate flame. SUBJECT is left to a *récit* or reinforced concreteness.

Concrete, *musique concrète*, pre-stressed space between *objets*. *Veshch Gegenstand Objet* voucher: an editorial to the international community in units or states. To undergo a terrace for a difference in pitch.

Pre-stressed concrete fortifies romance. From where we stand the chamber prefers serenity fragile. We walk toward the outcome of the project. CHANGE OF STATE.

Authority accrues to fame and so authority is ascribed to him he who is not the AUTHOR. Up the ramp of anticipating free-form to be a contested site. Allowing only the SUBJECT his o.k. we are preparing questions TEST that cannot be answered by Yes/No.

To inter to deposit a body in the earth to under an interval. CHANGE OF STATE SANCTION stare. To undergo a stare. To undergo a tonal object. To sound out an archive. To see or to meet an archaic smile.

2

What to do with a stranger?

> Bathe her and anoint her in oils, permit her to feast. Then interview her.

Then interview her

> Ask her name and from whence she came. Then how she came to this pass.
>
> This is a test.

This is a test.

END.

This is a test.

> Permit her to live in the strange land.

END

What to do with a stranger? Bathe her and anoint her in oils, permit her to feast.

Then interview her.

> SENDER is to issue a few central questions in advance, a preview to allow the
> SUBJECT a chance to think—I do not believe in ambushing the subject to achieve
> some sort of aggravated spontaneity. HELPER may indeed have three or four
> questions and fears. Also ours. A coincident prose.

Then interview her. Ask her name and from whence she came. Then how she came to this
> pass. This is a test.
>
> SENDER: What is the relation of drawing to either of these practices?

This is a test.

> SENDER One way to approach X's practice is to coax ratio, proportion, and
> measure through lavish phenomena manifest in the world of nature. Do you agree?

SENDER Then, too, the laws of probability inspire form. How does this work for X in practice: how does an equation for probabilistic situations translate into either spatial studies or sound scores?

SENDER Considering B's antipathy for X's approach to music, I wonder whether B ever had invited X to IRCOM in any capacity? SUBJECT [Any answer.] SANCTION
END.

This is a test. Permit her to live in the strange land.
SANCTION CHANGE OF STATE
END

What to do with a stranger? Bathe her and anoint her in oils, permit her to feast.
Then interview her.

SENDER is to issue a few central questions in advance to structure the interview to allow the SUBJECT a chance to think—I do not believe in provoking the subject to tilt some sort of misguided spontaneity in flight! HELPER may indeed issue three or four questions also and ours, kindred may overlay. **Infer her. Test test test test** coincidence of number **emitted in collapse.**

Then interview her. Ask her name and from whence she came. Then how she came to this pass.
This is a test. **Color code streaming protocols, invading camps**
SENDER: What is the relation of drawing to either of these practices?

This is a test. **Plot sound stream along y-axis**
SENDER To approach X's practice is to revoke ratio, proportion, and measure as laws of phenomena. Do you agree?

60

SENDER Then, too, the laws of probability inspire form. How does this work for X in practice: how does an equation for probabilistic situations translate into either spatial studies or sound scores? **Raise pulley. Stop wave.**

SENDER Considering B's antipathy for X's approach to music, I wonder whether B had ever invited X to IRCOM in any capacity? SUBJECT [Any answer.] SANCTION ateliers.

END.

This is a test. Permit her to live in the strange land.

SANCTION CHANGE OF STATE **Crack research over rock; hurl rock at research; rethink torrent.**

END

Then interview her.

Within sound of floor characteristics confer

Permit her to live as a stranger or do not permit her to live as a stranger

Figure 1: Osaka, 1956, gives a permit gives permissive flooring scheduled scan. To demonstrate irregular flooring a permit underfoot. If you are within the sound If you are circa 1956, Osaka, **Permit or Do Not Permit**, Park morpheme in festival, text only. Test test test flooring. **Pause.**

Glissandi per mit. Per mit per mute stranger to sound in a kinship with flooring, flooring's voice box and festival. Permeate flooring with voice. Per meate clay permit clay to sound. Sound out stranger, hurl stranger at strange clay although she would prefer to be anointed with minutes. A permit ting ting ting sound nearly next to inaudible. Inaudibly permeable business per mil. Prefer your research to mine. SEND in any capacity.

This is a test.

3

We pause. Ever smaller

transmissions lay in intervals i.e., *space between ramparts; more at* WALL

For family testimonials and tesserae SEE, MEET

Probability, a frequency.

Unrelated new relatives **vault incrementally—no, you** lie here in intervals; more at **EL**

For family **requiring an oath from shell** SEE, MEET **and mete out a pavilion.**

Probability **frequented.**

Any further thoughts? He paused: Algorithms?

Unrelenting new relatives lie here **resembling *an eternal die.***

For your family's elliptical references SEE, MEET **an era. The door slams.**

Probability **used as a ticket, tally, or voucher.**

We pause.

Probability, a frequency.

RECEIVE further looks. We pause.

Our bodies were brought to sanguinary **reverb**

at a WALL, antecedent and emitting soundscapes.

Probability, **frequencies of a** fragrance.

Independence **lived on, streaming glass**

cadenzas unrelated **to each other. Here lies a threat to plausibility.**

For family **test patterns** and tesserae SEE, MEET.

INVERLEITH HOUSE

Inverleith House

1

A quotient of narrative sentences

                  a stone

residence to become recitative suitable for art:

                         exempt it

from furnishings,

          expedite

avalanche, the light through which to walk through puddles and protons

and particularity, more like burnt staples

                      and attachments

than number in the abstract.

Stony syllables

         storied

            prospects

turned inward voluntarily, fairly filmed

puddles stapled to granular drive, intriguing

                     the way of examples

                          concrete splashing

throughout light's dot matrix.

              Errata are not universals

so they belong here

         clumped in puddles.

2

Plumbago

> *As botanical term*
>
> *Meaning of, for pencil lead*
>
> *See also graphite; Thoreau and Company*

He knew, he did not know

He knew, did not know then

The already known but not yet

Derived by him: one to three

Graphite to clay beguiled from

The crack of dawn.

It was generally assumed

Audio-visuals would have us bestow

The already known to him

Whom we know an object belonging

It had been assumed, ascribed

It had aubade written all over it.

. . . short sentences drawn from long experience.

Stylus

> *Evolution of shape*
>
> *Illustrated by Gesner*
>
> *With pointed and flattened ends*
>
> *Quality of mark of*
>
> *Violent use of*

3

      Solace

possible or accessible

            And requisite fingertips

of more or less the same surface differing only with respect to realism:

      inside out, for instance,

               subsonic

                  beyond;

      whether or not

           succulent.

Plastic or glass?

           Plastic.

               How so?

Plastic is warmer.

           Anything else?

Inverleith Use

In practice so that: *SO THAT:*

                    minus the furnishings.
Minus the furnishings would be one way
to wire a thoroughfare for controversy's emanations
about six times a year.

              Every few weeks, now and then
extract this evening's impatient pitch variations from time
immemorial, just then
the gallery empty.

           Disinclination thicker in the center.

ENTER the thoroughgoing table.
so that you may seize the resident,

                 banging its plenitude

                            a leaflet's late

footfall [from the] other direction.

                We thought

without signage then, with signage now.
Never did I read a letter
ENTER SO THAT: frequent frequency.

               We thought:

Put Heat Here. Radiant 1960 or so with radiators under
controvertible art, opening and closing up and

                     down

stairs: PUSH BAR. Bright day would be one way.
Minus the resident, says the residence, now thoroughgoing platform.

In practice so that: *SO THAT:*

                              disentangle furnishings

to extract attention

                        just then soon after that following next

                                      according to what

theoretical then and there.

ENTER the mix

                  so that you may seize the

syntax from another direction,

                        we thought

without signage then, with signage now.

SPACE BAR of locution and/or

                        eddying

stage for thoroughfare, we thought how to keep you

                                    from running away

en route to GO.

                Perhaps by offering a light,

a quotient of vicinity

                    instantiated, utmost, not undifferentiated.

How do you decide? Favorite color?

                      Alas, as is this deficit

among "egocentric wants" en route to what

STOP. IT GOES WITHOUT SAYING ought.

                              Might have a

leaflet.

Low volume happened.

                  Perhaps in arrears of tragic reversal,

all but one.

A pair of speakers is cold enough.

A small number grieve

                  move in parenthesis of she

who moves close, closest

                    inherits a conjecture.

YOUR RECEIPT.

               Fixing a look is an adherent turning to go.

THIS WAY OUT. Stops loosely stacked.

Another must regard her.

                  In an unusually effective pivot

someone OTHER THAN YOU vocalizes:

the interlocutor in the play speaks in fits and starts, starts and stops,

trial and error to his voice recording

                       whose self-regard is demonstrably lying still but all but abducted

up and down and from side to side.

                    We, a compendium.

Off the glare, without glare, under the glare of voice-over, is the partial past

pre-recorded.

            How does introducing a tape recorder on stage change things?

Up and down vintage lullaby

                  recollects a lyricism of which he is the lack.

                                   Pause.

Looking over his should scalding hot, he,

                  stepping back all the while,

fixes his gaze or rather cultivates

And that ye study to be quiet.

SO THAT you may seize recto/verso

                ought grafting other

regard for one. We thought signage. We thought a second glance

for fast forward in the gaze of stop, pause, where studio had been.

IT GOES via footfall: solitary

             solitaire

                solitude.

Thoroughgoing footfall

          PRIVATE thermostat

in residence.

       "I collect Beckett—up here" (POINT TO HEAD).

OCCUPIED veering habitat from VACANT heating units.

Under skull and wall

           washers, track lighting, mark PUBLIC access,

performance and commentary.

Inverleith H

The world of pavilion is the world's sound
   decomposing hale fades.
The world's sounding fades
  from mathematics.
Mathematics has spelt—spit out—spasmatic
  charcoal, the world of.
And we inhale phenomena. We, the world
   of smoke and thumps, approach property,
   inhaling plosives from botanics
   spirited and brave.
We inhale phenomena for which myopia is a nutrient.
Nutritious smoke! The world of probabilities.
Decaying amps effect a thermal sparkle.

PRESS BAR. "Gale" equals "a strong current."
Barrier tape botanica now modern
takes deep breaths depths in the iris and congress
   of a furnished past. Our days leave
   in a gale of ultraviolet.
Reset gale. OPEN at world. Proceed to event,
   eventualities and tape pressed to niceties
   furnish a wall with in situ
   sent from deep breaths.
HOURS rendezvous with eventualities. PRESS.

EX LIBRIS

1

INVITATION

SLIDE LECTURE

ARCHITECTURE

DR. HANS POELZIG

Light the phrase
Frequently

Backlit time
Of radio

Frequencies
That mostly take

Film, filmed inheritance

Documentary light

Frequent the object

From the onset of

Façade bathed in hindsight

And aftermath

The backlit referent is speaking

Retrospectively

We spun the face

Then we rotate face value

In its light assembly

Of eyeglasses, his aerial

We look forward to the facecloth

And frequent screens

We stare at ago

Ago's prodigal fold

Ago SAVE AS agon

Lit from

Le lecteur for he is

At a fast fade

Of eyes reflective

SAVE AS glare

Thought to equip futurity

No—to incite futurity

Can you hear me

Back thereness?

Ex Libris

Can you hear me

Back there

1926

OR

"So 'thereness'

is a protosemantically . . ."

divergent world.

Can you hear me

Back there

Thereness, there, thereness

AND

Thereness, tea-steeped

Pause. To whom . . .

Ex Libris

Estranged

                                                Field

Of vision

One event

Or two?

2

He had not yet built the building by which we best know him.

It shall have been written

        Any unbuilt events becoming true(r)?

        This site remains singularly occupied

        His die, his die already inscribed with . . .

        100% location—in perpetuity.

                        Thucyd.

        He was pronounced unbuilt

        Fame changes people into things and futures

        Enlightenment . . . will have been startled utopic drop cloth.

They wrote

        What of the what preconcert

                        are we

                              are we premature

                                          are we premature paper architecture

        Are we translating?

        Obit, Homeric

75

What's past is prologue.

Ancient evergreen

Antiquity for anticipation

In future "premature histories"

      (quoting her)

           (quoting her) hereafter

                  In Pompeii, sievelike

What might have slowed

Anon, tall dark and handsome as ever

Take care, kind passerby, maintain this tomb.

Audit past

An unbuilt sentence.

A future far-fetched and confiscated

      for which he will be known

             for which he will have been known futureshock

They wrote

      Rounded off (to) the nearest past

            functionally significant as earth

She broached

      He will die ten years later

      He will die on the eve of leaving for Ankara, a scar.

      He may have built a functionally significant fast forward blot

          flowering ungovernable marines

It shall have been written

      Any unbuilt events becoming truer

      quasi-aesthetic annals?

(The Undersigned)

      Unbuilt to themselves

(Signed)

Immortal Deixis, famished

3

Elevation: the century's flexing

narrative will have become fabula on axis with the

arisen interior

Rotunda. One steps through air floor to ceiling and within

the wall of glass, glass slowly pivots open: step down to a theory of rim.

Where?

Were there a reissue of the coin toss

to reinstate nonconformist

uneven odds underfoot melting with unkempt scherzo to the slope, we,

bequeathed exit, might again hesitate. Would have

Ex Libris

characteristic of her. Characteristic of them, the theory of.

He: Frankfurt is protective of her, having foreseen something.

She: No, Detroit, Frankfurt's muse, is . . . has seen something

marvelous: a calculus overlooking naught.

On/off.

The eye strides across the edifice.

The eye

strobes across the edifice.

Wish for open-air

hospital having been

innovative on these same lands and diagnostic

subsequently enstranged

in sought-for person on axis with falling action

much worse than arcade

proxemics. REWRITE

X and Y as low motion scroll in taxis and genera

much elevated

by the Helper, the Helper's cantilevered joke structure

to a footfall on the irregular ground as we

approaching solid and void

desire for breath.

Cleft to enunciate

exit, hesitate. Would have

the irregular ground as we.

Were there a reissue of the coin toss . . .

Sloping dye plant, growth thereof *in taxis.*

Cleft: joke effacement would have

inside-out point R on the tomb coinciding with vanishing

fabula on axis with

falter fast faster fasting.

REWRITE elevation.

4

Estate, we brought a family name GIVEN name taken from COUNTRY and acquired country of origin, a name that becomes HOME to a family of names, in property: THE PROPERTY OF_____

to divest itself, now being INHABITED of exceptional research. ON THIS SITE, housing

an estate, mental; financed by the doctor himself HE WHO GAVE he his to us our lives the sales from his children's book—say again: in HOSPITAL we were underwritten by the doctor whose psychiatric initiative it was to diagnose difference each with its own garden. Estate non-invasive ramified. LET US RAMIFY

Estate secured to the uprights of scaffolding to support the corridor INSTRUMENTAL in inaugurating international assiduity in thought, the crest of a hill the backbone, an architecture by him.

Estate: Chemical Plant Advances Research! Synthetic indigo, rubbing off diaries WHAT EARTHS ARE NOT LABORATORY

and industry, no longer hypothetical but categorical bait-and-switch SITE OF research to SICKEN INVALIDATE DISENTITLE ELIMINATE persons FACTORY.

Estate: evacuated, MILITARY HEADQUARTERS occupied then evacuated name then ENDED it. Vacancy.

Hiatus.

ESTATE: TO END off and on.

Estate TO SPRING OPEN research for ADVANCING neighbors: many names and other, we in studies that INTERMIX INTERMIT RECIPROCATE aporia INSTITUTE. Ongoing, wrote the edifice.

Estate: UNIVERSITY open to remembrance with all façade a document of prior history ON THIS SITE, walls ENGROSSED IN German/English English/German reference, thesaurus from the ground up

and, to CONFER vigilance,

estate to which gymnasium students come annually TO READ THIS LEGEND: At what iteration do notes become the drawing of explanatory force?

ASYLUM FOR INDETERMINACY

As though unintelligible, forests entertain humans as mere kindergarteners. Correlative

nature is a Babel; to nature humans are as simple as ABC. Correlatives: if nature appears

in READ ONLY, man appears ALREADY WRITTEN. Correlatives legible if

unintelligible is nature to man; to nature human nature is intelligible evidently.

Forests are synagogues polyglot to the man walking by, staring back. Walk-in signage

that issues from a provisional simultaneous Babel of want confronts us; put another way walk-in

signage that issues from function knows us better than we know it. At first a forest

bewildering to us, then a forest wild with possibility deciphers us as

novices amid growth. ENTER

EXIT   EXIT

EXIT yes, but   EXIT

To the Book. Meanwhile, I had had in mind
a featured mention,

EXIT yes, but   EXIT because
(for Žižek)   (For Habermas)

non-revocable mention make or revoke your objection the vocalizing
of recess or database of strike-throughs of strikes striking the base strikingly

EXIT yes, but   EXIT as if

fictive, the very page. They would disabuse us of identity irascible ink preferable
the fact the fact of ink's skittering microeconomics

in the long ennui.

We see the pillars of nature that stare back nature,

                                          knowingly

knowing more than we who notice.

We endure nature. We hear murmurs

                                    in temples gather

foreign stares of those entities.

EXIT

We endure nature, nature's staringly kindred pillars and authorship
of us.

        Introduced and edited by . . .

CORRESPONDENCES

ALLOW CONFUSED WORDS TO ARISE

GOES BY

OBSERVE

THROUGH FAMILIAR

CORRELATIVES

UTTER A BABEL OF WORDS

TRAVERSES IT

WATCH

WITH KNOWING

That's Russian . . . what does it say?

It says, KEEP THE REVOLUTION GOING!

                                       And ratchets

ALLOW CONFUSED WORDS TO ARISE

with what GOES BY glut and passeth away adequately

to OBSERVE much less effort

THROUGH FAMILIAR electronics: modernism

lightfast CORRELATIVES as body wrap.

UTTER A BABEL OF WORDS. Unsubscribe

Out-and-out gaming TRAVERSES IT

WATCH something that follows from emphasis

WITH KNOWING know-how, the cut somewhat earlier, tell her.

Tell her you've just sold one.

CORRESPONDENCES

ALLOW an asylum for indeterminacy *gay with rough moss*
to try signal-to-noise in a different sense of CONFUSED fascinated
confused, yet again.
WORDS TO ARISE in probabilistic lint

go by, GOES BY rate of change. Fans
OBSERVE "in the natural or original position," circa 1740. Herculaneum?
Chose One: "coteries," "blades" THROUGH FAMILIAR CORRELATIVES' inflatable zones
UTTERING A BABEL OF WORDS
"Hence the Pop twang and the anti-theoretical stance."

A dry-cleaning rack TRAVERSES IT somewhat like an assembly functionally derived,
to suspend a narrative on WATCH and
WITH KNOWING "things
the mind already knows."

Yes, but from where does HE come?
Water-soluble CONFUSION acquainted with studio practice
Be loquacious and mix with All Purpose, WORDS TO ARISE
THROUGHOUT routine consecutiveness, letter writing and agreement,
"we agree to disagree" being one.
As the sparks fly upwards.

EVENING HARMONY

CORRESPONDENCES
ALLOW CONFUSED WORDS TO ARISE

GOES BY
OBSERVE
THROUGH FAMILIAR

CORRELATIVES
UTTER A BABEL OF WORDS

TRAVERSE IT
WATCH
WITH KNOWING

A breathing spell GOES BY another name. As we OBSERVE abide by regard with regard to red ink and be related study respect as we seem to be irrelevant he looks irrelevantly at us through his deficit *please passerby take care and maintain this tomb of my beloved wife* face public scanning surveying the demographic and without regard for regimen as we are deemed irrelevant since not useful to her gaze and gaze at the reverse study the obverse peer stare THROUGH FAMILIAR intimate customary commonplace presumptuous CORRELATIVES. Intimate interchangeability. UTTER excitedly A BABEL OF WORDS heatedly or near. A mixture TRAVERSES IT. She danced with her back to us. Not on the back, there being no back WATCH this repulse, this detour danced At Arm's Length WITH KNOWING in the sense of "to acquaint oneself with" as concomitant to understanding, the reverb from tapping detected only by the detective.

Pass over: TRAVERSES and GOES BY a mind admit impediments "don't all rush me at once" Three Standard Stoppages curb divert deflect thwart frustrate deter mar obstruct stall Stop Restart press the play/pause button again refer to page 18 the display appears several seconds after the tray closes goes by runs its course runs out elapses tomorrow and glances at slight Will you not stay stop deflect your course to listen neglect negligence teaches what watchful senses lose sight of let slip forget oneself not give a thought to examine well your own thoughts WATCH OBSERVE inquiry Stop Caution Go vigilant at night alert through drowsy inactivity scan to mark for metrical something must nonetheless be surveyed for the exceptional and/or stealthy process or condition sharing a mammogram "we've been watching you for some time" and "under observation" share companion strokes pause (pause) goes off and (play) appears in Readies a jacquard of stops to scan to refer to starting from track 1 potential few if any some many all none meaning hot or stay where you are potential few if any incidences of unexploded minds and under the concept beneath to the eye the innocent eye postulates the primary order of observatories. Eeek! Humans! UTTER A BABEL or wrods to that effect—do you mean Hello? And yet the cut can be made with regard to legislating normative amps "Experiments by French physicists André-Marie Ampère and François Arago support Øersted's finding, establishing the concept of electromagnetism." Experimental wire, 1820, wire helix [also]. Any you? A history of attraction and repulsion wire helix acts like a paragraph when an electric current passes without qualification circa 1960 this is what people believe scientists believe "what constitutes a language" bring about Nous Parlons Zone We Speak Assemblage "scientific language in particular" re-runs Am I being clear? Unclear the Decks! CONFUSED TO ARISE families of verifiability tear down to teardowns also known as bring to ruin "Confuse" (archaic) "bring to ruin" real estate demo as demolition in urban renewal for Propylaen Now Appearing! Live and In Person to develop appearances pro-active in alliance with appearances propylaen livid—this is not what we meant by cosmopolitanism see Situationism exit enter quit portal marble slabs. Slab! Beam! But you know all that.

CORRESPONDENCES CORRELATIVES Under Construction! Idem The Same pronouns on tap Prouns on tap tap tap artificial languages still seize a congress of motives recursive stochastic superposition—why "especially"? "Equations that can describe large-scale phenomena" the music of 1952–53, a loose federation of quarrel but no index section plan selected edited and introduced plan introductions from which the above sets out presuppositions rendered problematic hence deserving of rewiring the entire mechanism May I introduce? fissures within the steel indicative of shattering on impact the cut here of forensic intimacy limits a seal plunged into cold wipe blade between each freeze heat freeze for immortal data Do Not Disturb application of belief to meaning ascertained it is said it is screamed is sung is constructed event being et cetera the words his companion emphatic pump One Event or Two? insurers' perspectivism give and take estate unanimously abstain absent split into ideological motive event eventual space time eventuality soon initiated relayed caught derived immediately in two hours time THROUGH FAMILIAR without having read rated under-read rendering of a as now a song stylist turned Sybil laminated without means other than no-nothingism Have a nice mesh—if only who what where when why WITH KNOWING at mid-term says J: "I'm thinking of forming a Committee of Public Safety" "Its motto: Read Or Die," says LMN, in a collateral inquiry with other tuning forks.

Hear it? a temp le giving off therm al

       sounds ands and wars wor words

in non-con templative crosstalk

from which catch phrases over phased have written

       to the point of of of unintelos

rust le and see m

       to catch sight of our odors y

yclept musk amber gris decay intimate

reunion of a skeptical sort

       with greenish greens taste tastes wood

the woods's ensemble e voc a tive.

THE SAME

Test positive for

evergreen.

Extrude correlative

life studies.

Voice correspondence

ultimately.

        Emit

the other dress.

Correspondences

Correlatives.

        A logic of,

pochade

ésquisse

        on or at Baudelaire's

spread sheet.

Spread

        a recursive iteration of

correlatives' textual frenzy.

Write obit,

        correspondence

such as signing, humming and whistling

itself
and its correlatives.
     Iterate decay.

Correspondences
Correlatives,
    a logic of
solitaire.

     Correspondingly solo
is your obit, whereas
decay correlates to his oboe's
sketch.

   Ocean, clear your throat.

Split to think.
Everything.

Solitary correlatives
solo correspondence

singular correlatives
correspondence, only
    broader:

"agreement of things with one another,"

"to be similar" or "to like" and "to give pleasure"

and/or

"phenomena or variables . . .

that which tend to vary or be associated together."

Her lightfast studies are not kind to articles

He attempted a gradient of withness and suchness.

Yes.

Whose enclosure? B looking underneath A

for pleasure, a) finds it, b) does not find it—

Yes?—

whereas B looks at D for corroboration,

fingering it. It escapes. B forfeits his turn.

FOR LORINE

The lesser the _____,
the greater the _____.

A test, for instance,
or a clue. Six across.

Within our non-stick forest
lives your ordinary forest

which, talkative,
unfailingly stares back

at the clumsy ear.
Heartlessness

is a sign
but a sign of what?

The ridicule.
The redicule.

OBELISK

1

A man shuffles past funerary cones and their admonitions

A man enters jungle of ciphers that deciphers him immediately.

Man enters a web of script.

Grottos of code give him a look.

A man jumps about a thicket of phonetics that penetrate.

Man enters calculus conversant with his gaze.

Through the revolving door are formula.

Nature is an acropolis on tap,

       a necropolis tapping out field songs the man walks through.

2.

Nature is a coliseum still breathing decibels

Nature is a covenant, is a synagogue issuing in nasal chromaticism.

Nature is a guide to period instruments.

Nature is an antiquariat.

Nature is a corridor livid with graffiti,

       a grotto vocalizing "Steal Away" in cipher.

Nature is a thesaurus in sing-song,

       a temple whose pillars transmit living memory partially.

Nature is an observatory emitting brilliance whose beam man breaks.

EVENING HARMONICS

Even after dusk slips away and into[1]   AFFLICTED wiring

darker aftermath electrifies[2]   units WOUNDED and disheveled

heat. Frequent infrared[3]   AS AN IMMENSE initiative.

Rafters vent light[4]   LIKE A VAST gray scale.

Darkest aftermath electrifies   units WOUNDED and disheveled.

footlights' delicacies extraordinary to   HUGE solar veto.

Rafters vent light   LIKE A VAST gray scale.

Who what where evenly lit[5]   CONGEALING individuals.

---

[1] Lyric effect. As here, "dusk" indicates the convention of in-between states of affairs and of mood, wherein symbolist chromaticism of affect loiters. Apparatus: style manual. Metalanguage: poetics.

[2] Nicola Tesla. Inventor of alternating current, Tesla sold his patent to General Electric, which used electricity to light the 1893 Chicago World's Fair. Tesla envisioned a world electrified.

[3] Infrared and technologies for photographing night scenes.

[4] Artificial lighting. Named for the inventor, Edison Avery Price became a conspicuous figure in inventing innovative lighting for modern museum display: wall washes, track lighting, and recessed ceiling fixtures being the most familiar.

[5] A sense of ending. Apart from the End's brilliant flash that brings closure or rebirth, aftermaths' fades represent philosophical remainders. How would lighting for remainders differ from lighting for quandariness?

Footlights' delicacies extraordinary to   HUGE solar veto

and antiseptic eventuality.[6]   She or he TREMBLES.

Wherefore megawatt   CONGEALING individuals

and lit in imitation of [7]   OWN COAGULATED throat.

Best antiseptic eventuality: she or he TREMBLES

in glare[8] ever after   chasing NOTHINGNESS, a sketch

lit a ticketed event in imitation of   your OWN COAGULATED throaty cortège.

Strobe aftereffect   THROBS ostensibly.

OWN COAGULATED

Here THROBS

AFFLICTED literature

VAST AND   NOTHINGNESS, undiagnosed

AS AN IMMENSE

TREMBLES

WOUNDED

HUGE unfalsifiable   VOID

LIKE A VAST abrasive

CONGEALING

---

[6]Abduction. Bringing certainty to investigation by degrees, abduction, C. S. Peirce might well say, is a term to invoke in the conservators' ongoing attempt to recuperate a late "black" painting by Ad Reinhardt from layers of damage and of prior restoration. Surprisingly, laser light passing over the painting breaks the chemical bond of sealant that then can be lifted from the surface. This technology is meant to counteract abrasive overcleaning of surfaces that destroys more than it restores.

[7] Theatrical lighting. In a footnote to Beckett's *Krapp's Last Tape*, the less necessary *Eh Joe* (staged as the fourth of "Beckett Shorts") displays the reruns' endless loop we call memory but more truly conveys a mode of self-justification in perpetuity. The actor sits immobile. To light for limbo Jennifer Tipton's solution is . . .

[8] Excess. Appropriately for a melodrama the Metropolitan Opera's production of *Sicilian Vespers* renders chiaroscuro hyperbolic.

TREMBLING metric scale

entering

threadbare pauses—and there

LIKE VAST gristle

CONGEALING

folded LIKE   VAST gristle

CONGEALING

one-eyed

and WOUNDED ink

that seems

COLOPHON

In the Futurity Lounge / Asylum for Indeterminacy was designed at Coffee House Press, in the historic Grain Belt Brewery's Bottling House near downtown Minneapolis. The text is set in Kinesis with titles in Futura.

FUNDER ACKNOWLEDGMENT

Coffee House Press is an independent nonprofit literary publisher. Our books are made possible through the generous support of grants and gifts from many foundations, corporate giving programs, state and federal support, and through donations from individuals who believe in the transformational power of literature. Coffee House Press receives major operating support from the Bush Foundation, the Jerome Foundation, the McKnight Foundation, from Target, and in part by a grant provided by the Minnesota State Arts Board, through an appropriation by the Minnesota State Legislature from the Minnesota Arts and Cultural Heritage Fund with money from the vote of the people of Minnesota on November 4, 2008, and a grant from the Wells Fargo Foundation of Minnesota. Coffee House also receives support from: several anonymous donors; Elmer L. and Eleanor J. Andersen Foundation; Suzanne Allen; Around Town Literary Media Guides; Patricia Beithon; Bill Berkson; the James L. and Nancy J. Bildner Foundation; the E. Thomas Binger and Rebecca Rand Fund of The Minneapolis Foundation; the Patrick and Aimee Butler Family Foundation; Ruth and Bruce Dayton; Dorsey & Whitney, LLP; Mary Ebert and Paul Stembler; Fredrikson & Byron, P.A.; Sally French; Jennifer Haugh; Anselm Hollo and Jane Dalrymple-Hollo; Jeffrey Hom; Carl and Heidi Horsch; Stephen and Isabel Keating; the Kenneth Koch Literary Estate; the Lenfestey Family Foundation; Ethan J. Litman; Carol and Aaron Mack; Mary McDermid; Sjur Midness and Briar Andresen; the Rehael Fund of the Minneapolis Foundation; Deborah Reynolds; Schwegman, Lundberg & Woessner, P.A.; John Sjoberg; David Smith; Kiki Smith; Mary Strand and Tom Fraser; Jeffrey Sugerman; Patricia Tilton; the Archie D. & Bertha H. Walker Foundation; Stu Wilson and Mel Barker; the Woessner Freeman Family Foundation; Margaret and Angus Wurtele; and many other generous individual donors.

To you and our many readers across the country, we send our thanks for your continuing support.

MISSION

The mission of Coffee House Press is to publish exciting, vital, and enduring authors of our time; to delight and inspire readers; to contribute to the cultural life of our community; and to enrich our literary heritage. By building on the best traditions of publishing and the book arts, we produce books that celebrate imagination, innovation in the craft of writing, and the many authentic voices of the American experience.

VISION

LITERATURE. We will promote literature as a vital art form, helping to redefine its role in contemporary life. We will publish authors whose groundbreaking work helps shape the direction of 21st-century literature.

WRITERS. We will foster the careers of our writers by making long-term commitments to their work, allowing them to take risks in form and content.

READERS. Readers of books we publish will experience new perspectives and an expanding intellectual landscape.

PUBLISHING. We will be leaders in developing a sustainable 21st-century model of independent literary publishing, pushing the boundaries of content, form, editing, audience development, and book technologies.

VALUES

Innovation and excellence in all activities

Diversity of people, ideas, and products

Advancing literary knowledge

Community through embracing many cultures

Ethical and highly professional management
and governance practices

Join us in our mission at coffeehousepress.org